YOUR RIGHT CAREER

HOW TO MAKE THE **RIGHT CHOICE** FOR YOUR **EDUCATION AND CAREER** PATH

LIVE THE LIFE YOU IMAGINE

BERNARD PERCY
WITH LEE EICHENBAUM

Published by
The Foundations of Brilliance
570 N. Rossmore Ave, Suite 105
Los Angeles, CA 90004

www.FoundationsOfBrilliance.com

Grateful acknowledgment is made to L. Ron Hubbard Library for permission to reproduce selections from the copyrighted works of L. Ron Hubbard.
IA # 17050801INT

ISBN 978-1546876786

TABLE OF CONTENTS

PREFACE

Why THE FOUNDATIONS OF BRILLIANCE?

After years of delivering the Foundations of Brilliance program to thousands of people in individual consultations, lectures and seminars I have no doubt that true brilliance resides within each and every one of us. The inspiration for this book has been the moments that moved me to tears seeing my clients shine like never before and the successes they have after completion of the consultation. It has been and continues to be my passion helping others find their dreams, and live the life they imagine. There is nothing better.

Thoreau wrote, *"Go confidently in the direction of your dreams and live the life you imagine."* Would you say, *"YES, I am going confidently in the direction of my dreams and living the life I imagine?"*

We have all heard the following statements:
"Find and go with your passion!"
"If I find my real purpose then life would be wonderful."

"Go with what you are really good at doing."
True, but not completely true. You must be able to truly answer the question, *"What is the right path for my career or education?"* To do this you would need to fully understand how to determine and align three factors of your success: your talents, personality, and purposes. It is not JUST your purposes, or personality, or talents taken individually. It is a method of addressing and aligning all three which gives the program the powerful results it achieves.

We think, *"If I could just find my purposes."* It's upsetting when we can't find them and joyous when we do. But having discovered one's purposes when the other two factors are missing doesn't guarantee happiness or success. All three factors are needed.

When I fully understood the power of the alignment of all three factors I began an intensive time developing a program to help people determine the path to achieve their TRUE professional or educational goals. The result of this effort is the FOUNDATIONS OF BRILLIANCE program.

I'm always exhilarated when a client fully realizes for themselves the professional or educational direction they truly want to pursue. This is often accompanied with tears from enlightenment and unburdening. Others laugh and laugh, others sit there with a pensive quietness. Whatever their reaction it is always that very special moment I look forward to and know will happen.

Helen Keller commented, *"One thing worse than not being able to see, is being able to see and having no vision."* The vision of what we want you to achieve is having the sense of fulfillment, satisfaction and self-respect that comes when you KNOW the educational or career path that is right for you.

UN-sure, UN-satisfied and UN-fulfilled should not be the result of the choices you make for your education or career paths.

Bernard Percy - Founder

Who is This Book For?

Winston Churchill commented, *"America will always do the right thing — after having exhausted all the possibilities."* By understanding fundamental principles about the key factors or components of success you won't have to exhaust all the possibilities in determining the education or career path that is best for you — no matter what age or where you are in creating your life. You will know with certainty and confidence that you are on the right path for you.

If the following are questions you are asking yourself, *this book is for you*:

- What is the professional or educational path that will result in the personal satisfaction, sense of fulfillment, and rewards I want from my work and study?
- Is the path I am on the one where I can truly achieve the brilliance and level of success I want?
- Am I doing what I am doing only because I am going along with what others are telling me to do and what is "best" for me?
- Am I experiencing the displeasure that comes from the daily grind of working in a job that brings little if any satisfaction and pride of accomplishment?

• How do I best create my remaining years of active life after retirement?

I asked a leading workforce development educator a question, *"How many of the students who are attending community colleges are really certain that they have chosen the educational or professional path that will provide them with a sense of fulfillment and satisfaction they want from their work or educational life?"* Her answer: *"Perhaps 5% are happy with their choice."*

Are you among that 5% group? Are you part of the 95% group not happy with your career or education choice?

Those not in that 5% group are often leading lives of quiet desperation and discontentment, or lives of boredom, resignation and dissatisfaction. Is that the life you want to have?

ACKNOWLEDGMENTS

I could spend pages of space acknowledging all the people who have helped and who have supported my efforts in creating and delivering the Foundations of Brilliance program, but in the interest of space I will only mention three:

The educators and other individuals throughout the world who are working tirelessly to create a better life for those they serve, and have supported my work with the Foundations of Brilliance.

Next, my partner and co-developer of the program, Lee Eichenbaum, whose contributions and support are greatly understood and appreciated. We are both Brooklyn boys, and love our friendship and our willingness to help create a better world.

And most importantly L. Ron Hubbard, educator, author and humanitarian. The program is based on his works and is the true foundation of the content and principles used in delivering this program. Without the writings and discoveries of

L. Ron Hubbard, the Foundations of Brilliance would not have become such a successful reality.

PART ONE
OVERVIEW AND INTRODUCTION

CHAPTER 1
WHAT DO YOU REALLY WANT TO PRODUCE IN LIFE?

> "If we asked ... 'What do you want to PRODUCE in life?' we could probably get a workable answer. From that he could figure out what he'd have to do to produce that and from that he could know what he had to BE. Then with a little cooperation, he would lead a happy and valuable life."
>
> *L. Ron Hubbard*

THE FOUNDATIONS OF BRILLIANCE BEGINNING

I originally developed the Foundations of Brilliance program to help high school students understand how to make the right decision about the education and professional path they would like to follow (and not have to exhaust all the possibilities before making the right decision). I wanted to help students determine where they truly wanted to be brilliant, and understand what is the right foundation on which to achieve that brilliance. Thus I called the program, The Foundations of Brilliance.

When I introduced parents to the program for their children, almost one for one the parent said, *"I need this, I want this for myself."*

The Foundations of Brilliance is intended to help you decide for yourself the professional or educational path that will help you live the career or educational life you imagine. The life that will bring you the ultimate sense of happiness and accomplishment, and with that the self-respect you deserve and desire to have.

This is true for 15 to 18 year old students who are really interested in finding the right educational path to follow. They are wondering should they go to college, what they should major in, what college should I go to, etc. Perhaps they are thinking of going right into the workforce and wondering what they should do.

It is also true if you are in the middle of your professional life and hit a glass ceiling or are unsatisfied with your career. It is true if you are about to retire or have just retired and want to determine what to do with the next 20 or more years of your life.

Someone I consulted sent me an email two years after completing the program. She thanked me for having changed her life and commented, *"You didn't make it easier, in fact, you helped make it more difficult, BUT MUCH MORE INTEREST-ING."* That brought a big smile to my face.

WHAT DO YOU REALLY WANT TO PRODUCE?

I heard a number that astounded me, there are over 150,000 books on the subject of helping you find your purposes in life, education, or profession. This is totally validated wherever I travel in the world by one of the most common questions and concerns, *"WHAT DO I REALLY WANT TO DO WITH MY LIFE."* But a much better question would be, *"WHAT DO I REALLY WANT TO PRODUCE WITH MY LIFE."* In a speech that played on YouTube, the speaker commented that he recently went to a reunion of classmates who graduated with him from Yale. They have all been very "success-ful" in their careers, many owning their own businesses, some were CEOs, lawyers, etc. The speaker commented that 80% of those who attended were not happy in how their careers had developed, even though they had achieved financial success, and were in high status positions. They felt they had a "wasted" life, and they were halfway through it.

They were not living a life founded on purpose, duty, and knowing what they really wanted to produce. Knowing what they really wanted to produce would lead them to know what they should DO for a career and what they should BE in that career.

NOTE: *Key terms to understand*

*To **produce** is to create a product, service or article; to bring into existence something that is of value such as a best selling book, a successful business, or products which improves a person's ability to learn.*

***Do** is defined as action, accomplishment, the attainment of goals and purposes. For example, the actions taken to make a financially successful business, making critically acclaimed works of art, educating children who are actively pursuing knowledge.*

***Be** is defined as choosing an identity, the role you are playing. For example: a businessman, an artist, a parent or an educator.*

*As a classroom teacher what I wanted to **produce** were students in pursuit of knowledge. I would **do** that by finding ways to challenge my students so they were in pursuit of knowledge and **be** a teacher who inspired them to action.*

The concept of duty is very important to many when choosing their career path. I was in Moldova (formerly a part of Romania) delivering a talk on principles of motivation to members of the Democratic Leadership group in that country. I asked the group to define the word "duty". A woman gave the best definition I have ever head, *"If not me, WHO?"*

This book will help you to understand how to clarify YOUR duty, and align that with your key factors of success to fulfill your dreams. Dreams based on the certainty of what you want to produce with the career path you have chosen.

ARE YOU AT A, B, C, OR D?

The following flow chart can help you determine where you are in relation to having a truly satisfying work and educational direction.

Where are you on the following diagram in terms of your educational or professional path, are you at A, B, C, or D?

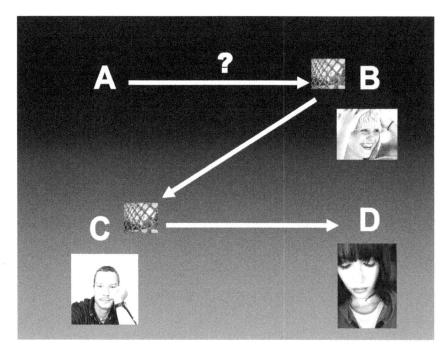

Point **A** is where you start to think about the best career or educational path to take. Some are stuck at **A**, we call them "wandering wonderers".

Point **B** is the IDEAL professional or educational path, where you have the SELF-RESPECT that accompanies being FOCUSED, PRODUCTIVE, and HAPPY in your work and studies!

Often barriers are hit in trying to get to the ideal, these barriers can be such things as money, resources, or perhaps most importantly not knowing with certainty what is your point **B**.

So you start moving to **C**, not the ideal, but it is OK. You are not particularly thrilled or happy, it is something you settled on doing. You have some satisfaction and sense of accomplishment, but really lack the true enthusiasm and joy you want from your job or education. And often barriers are hit in settling for **C**.

So you go to **D**. This is where you are VERY unsatisfied and unhappy in your work or studies. For seven years I was at a "**D**" job, getting very well paid. But I knew it was not the right professional path for me. I was very good at what I was doing, being a consultant developing training materials, documentation and marketing materials for high tech companies like Hewlett-Packard. I was making the most money I had ever made to that point in my life, but each day as I went to work I lost more and more *self-respect*. I was not really doing what I felt I was meant to do, but did not really know what that was or how to get to know what that was. I lived a constant life of unfulfillment about my career path.

Where are you at - A, B C or D?

CHAPTER 2
THE VISION — OR FROM RUGBY TO FASHION DESIGN

"Make your work to be in keeping with your purpose."

Leonardo da Vinci

DANIEL'S STORY
FROM RUGBY TO FASHION DESIGN

"Back in 2006 I did the Foundations of Brilliance program. At that time I had just completed the rugby season in Australia and was working out my plans for the future and what I wanted to do. My manager was working on my deal to go to France and play rugby there, and I had already started the motions to prepare for my visa. People were saying you should go, it will be the experience of a lifetime and I went along with it.

"I then did the program and as I did it I started to realize that I had been doing particular things my whole life and these things aligned with fashion. I was so excited about fashion that rugby took a back seat and I started creating my plans to take on the fashion world. I found my [career] basic purpose ..., it was always with me, but now I knew what it was thanks to the Foundations of Brilliance.

"This allowed me to align all my activities to this purpose and fashion was the game now. I told my manager that I was doing

fashion and I enrolled in fashion school. I traded the rough and tumble of rugby and the beautiful south of France for a crash course in fashion. My father being an ex-professional rugby player was very supportive of it and foot the bill for my tuition.

"With my basic purpose aligned with my actions, things took off. Eight years later my designs are now worn by the likes of Lenny Kravitz, Chris Brown, Usher, and Steven Tyler to name a few, and I am carried in high-end stores stretching from Los Angeles to Japan. I even have my own Flagship store in Los Angeles. It's rewarding to be on the right path where work is a pleasure and not actually work. The Foundations of Brilliance created this for me ..."

(You can go to www.danielpatrick.us/bio to see more about the successes Daniel is having.)

WHAT ARE YOUR "GARAGES"?

So many feel that determining the professional or educational path that will bring them the joy and satisfaction they seek is like going through hell. Winston Churchill commented, *"If you are going through hell ... keep on going."* If you are going through hell trying to find the right career you should just keep on going and find your way out of "hell".

Michael Hawley was with the MIT Media Lab when he related this anecdote about how the Smithsonian Museum created an exhibit to honor inventors and inventions (the Smithsonian Museum is a group of museums and research centers administered by the Government of the United States). A team was working to create the exhibit but could not agree on an organizing concept for the display. Finally someone suggested they contact Ray Bradbury, the renowned science fiction writer. They felt he would come up with an innova-

tive and appropriate concept they could all agree on. As Hawley told the story, Bradbury's response was that he would be willing to consult, with two non-negotiable conditions: First it would cost $100,000, and second, after he provided his advice there would be absolutely no further discussion or follow-up with him.

Being at an impasse and having an increasing necessity to come up with an organizing concept they agreed to Bradbury's terms.

When Bradbury met with them he first collected his $100,000. He then stated that after considerable thought he just had one word to say (reiterating that there would be no further discussion after he told them the word). He looked at the group who were waiting with incredulous disbelief, yet anxious with anticipation and interest. Some thought, *"$100,000 for one word, that better be a long word."*

He looked at the group and said, **"Garages!"** then left.

At first, you can imagine the word they wanted to use as Bradbury left. Then after considering what he meant, jeers turned to cheers. They thought about some of the greatest inventors and where they created their inventions — in their garages: the Wright brothers, Thomas Edison, Hewlett and Packard, Apple's founders Steve Jobs and Steve Wozniak, and so on. They finally knew what they had to do. **They found the vision for what they wanted to accomplish! They found their "garages".** They determined the answer that would help direct them to achieve the result they wanted, a way to honor American inventors and inventions.

When you know your "garages", you have the key understanding needed to achieve the results you desire. For example, one of my garages, one of my key understandings about raising my daughters, was that they know they are solvers of problems and were AmeriCANs, not AmeriCAN'Ts.

Do you know your "Garages"? What do you really want to produce? Your answer will provide the vision and help direct you to your right educational or professional path.

TO DO

1. What are your current garages, i.e., things that you are certain about in terms of your professional or educational path?

2. When you were younger, growing up with your future wide open to creation, what were your garages at that time?

3. Think of someone you are associated with and who is a person you believe has answered the question, "What is your garages?" Ask them, what are their garages, and why they chose that path?

For more information please go to www.foundationsofbrilliance.com and www.yourrightcareer.com

CHAPTER 3
ARE YOU IN PURSUIT OF KNOWLEDGE?

"A dream is in the mind of the believer, and in the hands of the doer. You are not given a dream, without being given the power to make it come true."

Unknown

HELPING REBECCA

Rebecca had started her freshman year in college. Ever since she was 8 years old she wanted to be a nurse. When she started college and had to select a major area of study, almost without thinking she wrote "nursing" and started her studies. After many sleepless nights, anxious days, and difficulties in studying she realized nursing was not the right career choice for her.

A question that kept running through her mind was, *"If I am this unhappy now with nursing, how will I feel about it in five years and will I regret having become a nurse?"*

She started an internal discussion with herself, *"Perhaps teaching, or sports administration, or maybe re-looking at being a nurse."* She tentatively decided on teaching high school English — she had teachers she really liked who had helped her when she was in school; they loved working with children. But lingering in her universe was the question, *"Is this what I really want to do for a profession?"* She was not certain and was concerned that she would be "wasting" more time in a major area of study that was not what she really wanted to do.

Like so many she tried to make an *educated guess* on what would be best for her:

"I like kids."

"Other teachers helped me a lot and I would like to help others."

"I like reading and literature, so I guess I should be a high school English teacher."

Rebecca was better than most. She at least had some idea about what she wanted to do and why. But she was not certain.

The questions became, *"How should I determine what I REALLY want to major in?"*

To determine what they REALLY want to do some people may try:

 Prayer.

 Others may go skydiving and not even confront the decision.

Others may go around in never ending circles trying to figure it all out.

And some get it right. This is Doris Bell, my mother-in-law, who at 90 was still working over 30 hours a week at her business. She owned a funeral home. She was "mom" to those who needed a caring, truly empathetic person to help comfort them after the loss of someone they loved.

But so many get it wrong. We hope the pilot of your next flight didn't, or the surgeon operating on someone you love didn't.

Working with Rebecca, we found the direction in her professional activity that inspired her, one that aligned with her talent, personality and purposes. She realized with certainty what she really wanted to achieve was *"To open people's eyes."* What better purpose could there be for a teacher. She now KNEW!

George Bernard Shaw wrote, *"What we want to achieve is the child in pursuit of knowledge, not knowledge in pursuit of the child."*

My professional life of over 50 years has been involved with education. I have had books published, was editor in chief of an award winning education magazine, traveled the world lecturing and consulting, and raised my three daughters. All with a focus to help individuals understand and strongly pursue knowledge to achieve their dreams of being brilliant and successful in the area of their chosen education or professional path. This is what happens when knowing what they want to produce, and following a purpose they agree with, that aligns with their talent and personality.

We have to recognize the world is constantly changing. When I was a young boy of about eight or nine, I remember the wonderful anticipation I felt waiting to receive the Roy Rogers ring I had ordered. (Roy Rogers was a cowboy TV star in the 1950s.) When the ring finally arrived it was a great and exciting moment in my life. The ring was made with cheap plastic, with an image of Roy Rogers on it. But to me it was a VERY special moment - I was truly happy. Today that ring would be very cheap and have no appeal to me if I were eight years old; times have indeed changed.

The world of work has also changed as the technology and possibilities in how we can create our lives have changed. What is vital to living a life of happiness, satisfaction and fulfillment is to make the right decisions about the education and professional path you will follow; knowing that your decisions may change as the world around you changes.

There's one finding of a report[1] by *McKinsey on Society*, an online forum for the consulting firm's research on pressing social issues. Among the findings in the study were that half of all graduates said they would pick a different major area of study or school if they had to do it all over again.

Are you working in the area you studied in school?

---

[1] Mckinsey & Company - Voice of the Graduate May 2013

It has been reported that those entering the workforce today will have up to 10 different professional paths during their working life. How can you choose the right path to take? These are issues and concerns that must be realized and solved.

TO DO

1. What are three or more things that inspire or inspired you to be in pursuit of knowledge?

2. How many different professional or educational pursuits have you had, or seriously thought about doing?

3. Can you predict with a good measure of certainty, what you will be doing five years from the day you read this page?

4. Do you have an idea of what you would love to be doing one year from the day you read this page?

For more information please go to www.foundationsofbrilliance.com and www.yourrightcareer.com

PART TWO
SELF
UNDERSTANDING

CHAPTER 4
A KEY BARRIER TO OVERCOME

"To love what you do and feel that it matters
— how could anything be more fun?"

Katharine Graham

DAVID'S STORY
SOARING TO NEW HEIGHTS

"I met Mr. Percy many years ago while in college. As a pioneer of assisting any and all to find their purpose Mr. Percy to date has been all over the world doing such.

"I feel very fortunate to have met him and done his program, the Foundations of Brilliance. This helps people find out what their [career] purpose is. What do you want to do? What are you meant to do? What specific talents, skills and abilities do you have? And moreover what is in your heart to do?

"This was — as it has been for many — a shock to me, people seem to have trouble with this or just don't know.

"I've talked to them about it. And I get answers like 'I don't know what I want to do', or they are done with school and still don't know, or worse just [want to] do something.

"Mr. Percy helps YOU figure this out. He is a very special caring person who being a man of this nature, does this lifelong quest of 'helping people'.

"I feel from doing this program, that I was able to see what I wanted to do. I learned more about myself, what I truly want to do/accomplish and BE.

"I have always wanted to be a pilot. Flying is my dream. But I

just could never seem to get there. It was as though I was always being detoured around my dream.

"I am now a professional pilot. I fly for a living! This joy of reaching and becoming what I wanted to do so long ago when I was first looking into the skies and seeing jets as they make streaks across the big blue [has come true]. I am now on my way.

"I want to thank Mr. Percy for his guidance and assistance in my personal dream.

"To you reading this, when you reach such a plateau you will understand what I mean, when I thank him."

THE FIXED IDEA AND SHAMPOOING MY HAIR

"A fixed idea is something accepted without personal inspection or agreement. It is the perfect 'authority knows best.' It is 'the reliable source'." L. Ron Hubbard

A fixed idea is an idea you think with and believe because that's the way it has always been done, or everyone knows that is the way things should be. You never really stop to determine:

- "Does that really make sense?"
- "Is that really the best way to do things?"
- "Is that really true?"

It can result in one being wooden-headed, or to be blunt "stupid" about something and acting without good judgment.

Here is an example of a fixed idea. Why do high schools typically teach the sciences in the order of biology, then chemistry, then physics? *Because of a fixed idea.* In the early 1900s there was a debate about the order in which the sciences should be taught and no consensus could be reached. Finally it was decided to teach them in alphabetical order, no other educational justification: first biology, then chemistry, then physics. Yet educators familiar with the sciences comment that physics should be taught first as it forms the foundation of knowledge on which to build an understanding of the other sciences.

Ideas that you have truly inspected, evaluated and determined its truth (or untruth) are your beliefs, they are NOT fixed ideas; those evaluated ideas can become your principles, your core beliefs. Ideas that are just accepted without evaluation can become fixed ideas.

For example, all my life I shampooed my hair twice. Why? When I was a little boy my mother told me to shampoo my hair twice (and you have to trust your mother don't you, she is your reliable source). Also the directions on the shampoo bottle said, *"Shampoo your hair, rinse, then repeat,"* and you have to always trust the authority don't you? But, isn't this really mainly a marketing concept to get you to buy more shampoo?

I had been shampooing twice my entire life, even though after one shampooing my hair is squeaky clean.

One day I resolved that I would only shampoo once; I must admit that was one of the hardest, most uncomfortable things I have ever done!

After my first shampooing and rinse, I turned off the water and walked out of the shower, but that felt so uncomfortable I had to rush back into the shower. Then I thought, *"NO, I am only shampooing once today!"* and walked out of the shower. Then felt I had to go back in, which I did — I had to shampoo twice. Finally I just ran out of the bathroom dripping wet. All day I checked my hair to feel if it was clean. Now I am able to easily shampoo once or if needed twice, I now have good judgment after spotting my fixed idea.

How many fixed ideas permeate our everyday life, ideas that direct our actions and our judgement; yet when evaluated make little or no sense? Superstitions are really nothing more than fixed ideas. For example, break a mirror and it is seven years of bad luck. A friend of mine told his mother when he was seven years old, *"I want to die now."* His mother was horrified and asked why. He answered, *"I have broken so many mirrors, my life is over. I will only have bad luck all my life!"* This is a true example of a fixed idea.

What are the fixed ideas that are found in your professional or educational decisions? Are there ideas, policies, beliefs, approaches that you may have or follow all the time. Have you wondered about or thought they seem to be contrary to what would be optimum or ideal?

It may not be easy to spot or change your accepted fixed ideas, yet you do need to constantly evaluate and ask, "Is that idea, policy, belief or approach truly best for me in determining my professional or educational path?"

What, if anything needs to be changed?

Here, for me, is an example of a professional fixed idea: *"That is a man's job — or a woman's job."*

What is the fixed idea the person loading the truck had? What are the probable dangers and problems just waiting to happen?

I must admit I still, with all my knowledge and beliefs, am surprised a bit when I see male nurses; I grew up "knowing" nursing was a woman's job.

When I was 12 ycars old I was waiting for a train on a subway station in New York City. I saw a janitor mopping the floor of the station. I was raised in a family and culture that valued education and the emphasis and expectations was always on having a profession that required a strong educational background. I was expected to go to college and become a professional or become involved in business. I thought to myself, who will be around to mop the floor in a few years? I "knew" everyone will become a professional in a highly skilled or valued profession, such as a doctor, teacher, business owner, manager, etc., and there will be no one left to mop the floors. A true fixed idea!

EXAMPLES OF WOODEN-HEADEDNESS AND FIXED IDEAS

Mark Twain said it best when he likened educational reform to moving a cemetery, observing, *"... it's difficult to persuade the inhabitants to pick up and move."* And we could say that about most efforts to reform any area of life. This can also be true for those who based their decisions and actions on wooden-headedness.

Wooden-headedness is based on fixed ideas that have not been evaluated or inspected, they are things agreed to because "that's just the way things are supposed to be." It is the source of self-deception, it consists of assessing a situation in terms of preconceived fixed notions while ignoring or rejecting any contrary signs.

Here are some examples of wooden-headedness that I have observed that stop someone from following a path that would bring fulfillment, happiness and self-respect:

- If the job pays well enough it doesn't matter what it is.
- I am pursuing my dreams/purposes/goals not in my job but elsewhere, therefore the job could be anything.
- I also have to live my life not only work. (They mean usually hobbies, traveling, having fun, as living their life.)
- My goal is to be financially independent and to have passive income (such as multilevel marketing). But they don't know what they are going to do when they become financially independent and what is the purpose behind it.
- Some think they would be happy if life would be a big vacation (like traveling, laying in the sun on the beach, etc.).
- Some think that finding their purpose belongs to philosophy and is not something which is practical and really useful.
- The inability or barrier I have is just exactly what makes it impossible for me to achieve what I want. For example, I don't have enough time, money or experience.
- A job that is just OK, is fine. I don't need better than that.
- I have to continue the family business.
- I have to make money because I need money first to be able to do what I really want to do.
- I need a college education to be successful.
- I should do what my parents tell me to do.
- I do a job only for the money, which provides the status I want.
- I want a job for the prestige.
- The husband must make more money than the wife.

Are you being wooden-headed in terms of your profession or education? Are there things you hold to be important, and perhaps even sacred mainly because everybody knows and understands "that is the way things are supposed to be"?

BUT, when these ideas are finally evaluated and inspected they may turn out NOT to be that important; or things which at first seemed unimportant and having little value turn out to be of major significance.

NOTE: I want to stress again, a belief that you have personally evaluated and inspected and found to be true for you, or not true, right for you or not right, is different then a wooden-headed fixed idea. For example, that sacred cow *"One needs a college education to be successful in life."* Of course this is true if one wants to be a doctor, a lawyer, etc., but how many people who studied something in college are still working in that field? As stated earlier, less than 50% are following the career path they determined in college.

TO DO

1. Is there some educational or professional path that you have thought, *"That is not for me!"*, ONLY because of a fixed idea, because everyone knows that is not a path to take for a person in my situation?

2. Is there a time when you have succeeded in something because you did it your way, and gone against what you were told by others was wrong for you?

3. Write about some education or professional paths that interest you, or were of interest to you without putting any attention on what others may think is the right thing for you to do?

For more information please go to www.foundationsofbrilliance.com and www.yourrightcareer.com

CHAPTER 5
IT DOESN'T TAKE COURAGE TO LIVE A LIFE TRUE TO YOURSELF

> "I wish I'd had the courage to live a life true to myself, not the life others expected of me."
>
> *Unknown*

One result of the Foundations of Brilliance consultation is the book Jeanne had been wanting to write for years, living a life true to herself: *The Modern Rapunzel — Natural Secrets for Ending Hair Loss and other Miracles. www.themodernrapunzel.com* .

JEANNE'S SUCCESS
"NOW EVERY DAY I AM LIVING MY DREAM."

"Several years ago I had the privilege of receiving the Foundations of Brilliance Program from Bernard Percy, himself!

"Discovering my talents, personality and purposes was an adventure and a life-changing experience. The line of questions asked steered me to a powerful moment of revelation and insight which led to my professional path revealing itself. Before that time the life force that surged in me was going into the air, un-manifested in the real world. I seemed to 'somewhat, somehow, sorta' find occupations that interested me but were on the fringe of the real game for me where I could truly shine.

"Now one of my purposes is to help women shine as the unique and special individuals they are, thus enabling them to express themselves in life according to their own wishes.

"Now every day I am living my dream, getting better and better at what I love to do and wake up every day not only excited but know I am making a dramatic difference in the world. I am an unstoppable force of pure purpose. Life is beautiful and sparkling like a diamond.

"With enormous gratitude and love."

A Cup of Goulash — A Symbol of Courage?

Why am I showing you this photo of a cup of Goulash and using that as a symbol of courage? Well, it is NOT a symbol of courage, it is a bowl of Goulash — a bowl that I ordered

while traveling first class on a train from Munich to Budapest. Just as a cup of Goulash does not symbolize courage, living a life true to yourself does not require courage; it requires an understanding of yourself to make the right decisions.

Courage is defined as the ability to do something that frightens one. One becomes frightened in the face of uncertainty and lack of belief in one's ability to overcome obstacles and barriers. Living a life true to yourself does not require courage; it requires a certainty that you know what is true for you, and the confidence and belief that you can make your dreams become a reality.

I met a very successful real estate investor who believed in her ability to help others know how to invest in real estate. When she started her company she had no experience investing other people's money, only a belief in herself. She was willing to pursue her dream to the point where she had less than $100 in her bank account. She went to the bank to withdraw her last money so she could buy food to eat, and when she went to withdraw the money she was told she had $20,100 in her account — she was shocked. One of her potential investors deposited the money in her account so she could start working with him. And today she is a millionaire. She had the belief in herself to pursue her dream in spite of it all.

As I was riding on the train from Munich I kept seeing views that were beautiful and even inspiring.

As you face the future where you know, with certainty, the path that is truly the right career choice for you, and truly believe you can bring your dreams to reality, you can see a view that is both beautiful and inspiring. It does NOT TAKE COURAGE to travel on that path. It does take a willingness to overcome the barriers and obstacles you may face as you move in the direction you have decided.

When I was teaching in New York City new teachers generally had a great deal of difficulty in their first weeks as a teacher. That difficulty often lasted for months or resulted in many giving up their dream to teach. As a "seasoned" pro I could usually tell who would do well and who would have great problems, and I was generally right. But then there were those who totally surprised me.

Sandi was one of the GREAT surprises. She was short, a bit on the heavy side, and did not appear to be a very strong personality. But when she got in front of her class she exuded confidence, ability and certainty, and from the very first day she could control her class and achieve her goals as a teacher.

Over the years I have been able to make my dreams become a reality. I have been traveling the world helping others to determine what is the best path for them to take to fulfill THEIR true dreams. Along the way I have enjoyed Goulash and breathtaking views. It did not require courage, it required certainty and belief in my ability to fulfill my dreams.

The Foundations of Brilliance helps create the foundation so that you know what YOU EXPECT OF YOU, and a belief in your ability to achieve your expectations.

TO DO

1. How can you apply this quote to your life?
"I wish I'd had the courage to live a life true to myself, not the life others expected of me."

2. What are three areas where you have the confidence and ability to achieve your goals?

3. What is an area(s) where you displayed the confidence and ability needed to achieve your goal(s)?

For more information please go to www.foundationsofbrilliance.com
and www.yourrightcareer.com

CHAPTER 6

IS SUCCESS A JOURNEY OR REACHING A DESTINATION?

> "Success is a journey, not a destination.
> The doing is often more important than
> the outcome."
>
> *Arthur Ashe*

I highly respect Arthur Ashe (a former tennis champion), he was truly a person to be admired and honored. I came up with a quote that I believe is very relevant, *"When you make a decision about what you want to do, you are really deciding what challenges you are willing to confront and handle."* If the journey involves confronting and overcoming the challenges YOU WANT TO FACE, then yes, successfully overcoming the challenges is definitely a success on the way to a destination.

But what if the journey involves challenges that are not really the ones you welcome, or do not succeed at overcoming, then is that journey a success?

LYNNE'S SUCCESS
A FABULOUS GAME OF LIFE

"Since doing the program with Bernard, I have had a TV show which ran once a week for a month and I do believe that it helped my reputation in this area as the artist and teacher I am. I have steadily expanded my teaching and also have secured more painting commissions.

"It was the total right thing to do and I really think it would be marvelous if everyone realized and saw their purpose clearly. And that others would see it too. Then the game of life would be quite fabulous indeed!"

To this rock climber, as he finds the right foot and handholds he is having success each step of the way, and it is certainly a success when he makes it to the top of his climb. (This is NOT a journey I care to take, and the thought of traveling on this path is the farthest thing from my mind.)

To be successful means to truly want to reach a destination that involves the challenges you are willing and able to overcome.

Ask yourself the following questions:

- Are you gladly facing the challenges you want to have as you move towards your destination in your education or work?

- Are you shaping and creating the challenges you know will help you arrive at your desired destination?

- Are you going in the direction of your dreams; are you on the right path to creating your future?

As I write this chapter, I am on a plane flying to Russia for a month. I am delivering consultations, seminars, and workshops on a variety of topics including the Foundations of Brilliance, parenting and education. I love the challenge of delivering so many different events and presentations; it fuels my desire to impact others in ways that help them achieve their dreams. My journey is in the right direction with the challenges that are right for me!

TO DO

1. Write about what you really enjoy doing.

2. Write about the types of challenges that you are willing to confront and overcome in the activities mentioned above.

3. What is it that gives you joy in succeeding at overcoming those challenges?

For more information please go to www.foundationsofbrilliance.com and www.yourrightcareer.com

CHAPTER 7
ONE STEP IN THE RIGHT DIRECTION

> "A journey of a thousand miles must begin with a single step."
>
> *Lao Tze*

The quote *"A journey of a thousand miles must begin with a single step"* is a great quote, but there is one question you need to answer before you take that single step, *"In which direction do you want to go?"* Knowing the correct answer to that question is so often the problem. If you take that first step in a wrong direction, your journey of a 1000 miles will take you 1000 miles in the WRONG direction.

TANII'S SUCCESS
A JOURNEY IN THE RIGHT DIRECTION

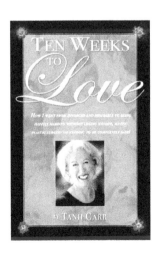

"Doing the Foundations of Brilliance program changed my life. Even as an adult, I wasn't sure what professional path would best utilize my skills and talents, but also fulfill my purposes beyond making money. I have several talents: writer, public speaker, singer, public relations. But I always thought I had to choose between them; it was always this OR that OR that. I could never make up my mind.

"When I did the program, I discovered something amazing! All of my skills, talents, passions were aligned and could be used to fulfill my life goals! No more "or" about anything. Everything fit beautifully!

"As a result of doing the program I published my first book, _Ten Weeks to Love_ (_www.10weeks2love.com_), with two other non-fiction books in the works, along with other 'Ten Weeks' products (CDs, DVDs, seminars, retreats). I've become a professional speaker, soon to be accepted as a member of the prestigious National Speaker's Association.

"I've done many radio shows as well as cutting a short demo CD of me singing with a world-class jazz pianist and songwriter, produced by a Grammy-winning sound engineer. I found my dream horse who has helped me connect with more people who are now interested in my book and speaking engagements.

"If someone would have told me before that all this could be achieved, I wouldn't have believed it. Believe it! I'm having the time of my life and wish the same for you!"

There are amazing stories of animals knowing what is the right path or direction to take. Salmon are able to return to the streams where they were born after spending years swimming in the ocean. They return to the same stream traveling enormous distances so they can lay their eggs to help create a new generation of salmon.

How do they know what direction to take and begin their journey that begins with a single motion of their fins?

One theory is that salmon use special magnetic navigation to figure out which way to travel. And when they arrive at the mouth of the stream that leads to the place where they were born, they are able to smell the stream's special scents, following these scents to their birthplace.

The story of how swallows fly over 12,000 miles round-trip from their winter home in Argentina and travel to Southern California, arriving at the Mission of Capistrano is very well known. What do these birds have to know to fly in the right direction to arrive at their true destination?

What must you know and understand about yourself to help you "travel" in the right direction for your educational or professional life? A life where you can, *"Confidently go in the direction of your dreams, and live the life you imagine."*

As discussed earlier there are really three basic factors to understand: your talents, your personality, and your purposes. You need to understand and gain certainty about these factors so you can begin your journey of a thousand miles with one step, IN THE RIGHT DIRECTION. Part Three in the book will help you achieve an understanding on how to determine this for yourself.

TO DO

1. Write about some ideas you have about the right direction to take.

2. When did you have the certainty that you were traveling in the right direction in some area of your life?

3. Who do you know that is traveling in the right direction? What do they understand about themselves that makes that possible?

After reading Part Three of the book, revisit what you just wrote and see if your ideas have changed.

For more information please go to www.foundationsofbrilliance.com
and www.yourrightcareer.com

CHAPTER 8
How Old do You Feel?

> "It is not true you stop pursuing dreams when you grow old. You grow old when you stop pursuing dreams."
>
> *Alfonso Molina*

NIKKI'S SUCCESS
ONCE AGAIN EXCITED FOR MY FUTURE

"I've always been artsy and had a passion for animals and science but I wasn't really able to quite piece things together so perfectly until I did the Foundations of Brilliance program. I fell into the field of accounting as a result of losing direction by allowing outside influences to direct me to what I "should" do for a living. I wasted three to four years dreading getting up in the morning for work.

"Once I did this program, everything became clear! I am currently sitting in Heathrow Airport on my way to New Delhi. I am bringing my camera and untamed spirit along with me. I am finally going for what I have always wanted — international traveler and photographer.

"My next trip will be focused on volunteering with international wildlife conservation efforts. Once back in the U.S., I plan to

study Wildlife Biology and Animal Behavior, eventually pursuing a graduate degree abroad. Just two months ago I was sitting at a computer in a cubicle.

"Foundations of Brilliance has drastically changed my life and I am so happy to say that I am once again excited for my future!"

IS THIS THE REAL FOUNTAIN OF YOUTH?

For me there is potential magic in the above quote from Alfonso Molina. This quote is a source of youthful feeling and zest for life, a fountain of youth. Every once in a while we hit a wall, we lose, we fail, we hear the word "no" too many times. We feel stopped by our family, our colleagues, our environment; then we begin to feel old (no matter our actual age). At those times let's revisit our dreams, let's continue in the pursuit of those dreams, let's stay young.

If you said to me in 1965 as I started my professional journey through life that I would have led the life I am living, I would have told you, *"You are crazy."* I knew I would have 2 or 3 children, live in an apartment in Brooklyn, drive a Volvo and lead a "normal" middle class life as a teacher in New York City public schools.

But there has been one constant that has followed me throughout my life, the willingness and ability to reinvent myself.

1976 was the last year that I was a full time classroom teacher, and ever since then I have found that I have been reinventing myself and my professional career every 5 to 7 years. I am always using what I have done previously as a foundation to succeed. I must admit I occasionally wished that I had led a more comfortable, conservative and predictable life, but those are only momentary thoughts. It is my nature, my personality, to seek to reinvent myself and grow as a person as I undertake new challenges to reach new horizons.

As life expectancy increases throughout the world, adults who are retiring from their full time careers will have many years of productive time to reinvent themselves. (If you live in Monaco the overall life expectancy would be 87.2 years, in Canada 83.5 years, in the United States, 79.8 years.) The question becomes for those in retirement age, *"How should I reinvent myself and do something fulfilling and rewarding as I create the next phase of my life?"*

Below are a couple of relevant quotes that communicate the value and importance of reinventing yourself, especially in those potentially very purposeful and productive years after retirement. As you read these quotes answer the questions that follow:

> "People who cannot invent and reinvent themselves must be content with borrowed postures, secondhand ideas, fitting in instead of standing out."
> *Warren G. Bennis*

Are you willing and able to reinvent yourself?

> "It's impossible," said pride. "It's risky," said experience. "It's pointless," said reason. "Give it a try," whispered the HEART."
> *Unknown*

What does your heart tell you to do?

> "There is no passion to be found in settling for a life that is less than the one you are capable of living."
> *Nelson Mandela*

Are you living the life you are capable of living?

> "The future belongs to those who believe in the beauty of their dreams."
> *Eleanor Roosevelt*

Are you creating a future for yourself and believe in the beauty of your dreams?

> "You can't start the next chapter of your life if you keep re-reading the last one."
> *Unknown*

Are you looking at what you want to do with the next chapter(s) of your life? Too many people get stuck in the past. It is true that one can learn lessons from their past, but you must be willing to look forward and write the next chapter.

The Foundations of Brilliance program helps you choose the right path to take as you reinvent yourself to lead a valuable and rewarding life. And discover your fountain of youth.

TO DO

1. Are you growing old or are you staying young?

2. Do you know and are you still pursuing your professional or educational dreams?

3. Or, have you stopped pursuing those dreams because _____?

4. How willing are you to create new dreams to pursue?

5. Or do you think with a "what's the use" mentality?

6. Do you dare to dream large dreams, or do you confine yourself to small ones because _____ ?

7. Who are the most vital and energetic people you know or have met? What are the dreams they are pursuing?

8. Will you drink from the fountain of youth and stay young or grow old ? **YOUR CHOICE**

9. Take a couple of moments and write out the dreams, the big dreams, you truly want to pursue and you know you want to achieve by believing in the beauty of those dreams.

PART THREE
The Three Key
Success Factors

NOTE: This next section is intended to provide you with an understanding of what you need to know about yourself to determine the educational and career path that is best for you. Some of you may decide you need additional assistance from a consultant trained to deliver the Foundations of Brilliance program. If you need any further assistance, or if you have any questions or comments, please send us an email at bernard@yourrightcareer.com or lee@yourrightcareer.com.

CHAPTER 9

UNDERSTANDING THE FOUNDATIONS OF BRILLIANCE PROGRAM

> "Talent, and inherent personality and basic purpose go together as a package."
>
> *L. Ron Hubbard*

CAROLINE'S STORY
STEERED IN THE RIGHT DIRECTION

"My life has become steeped in music — I can't think of a more wonderful situation. My five piano students are doing very well. [Knowing the basics of how students study and learn] and together with my technical piano skills seem to be a good combination. We just completed a spring musical, a production of Finian's Rainbow *— truly a delightful experience for students, parents, audiences and those of us directing.*

"Thanks again for your help steering me in the right direction Bernard. I knew years ago that I had to put being a music professional on the back burner as I couldn't stand up to the suppression in the field. There was quite a process of extricating myself from the false purposes, and you were certainly key to that process. Now I work in the area where I have skill, ability, love, talent, joy and, of course, purpose.

"Thank you once more, dear friend, for your help."

Let's review the following diagram which first appeared in Chapter 1. Where are you on the following diagram in terms of your educational or professional path, are you at A, B, C, or D?

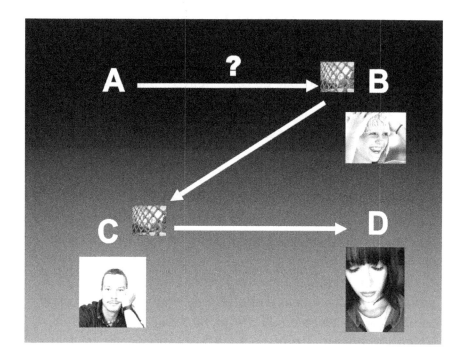

Point **A** is where you start to think about the best professional or educational path to take. Some are stuck at **A**, we call them "wandering wonderers".

Point **B** is the IDEAL professional or educational path, where you have the SELF-RESPECT that accompanies being FOCUSED, PRODUCTIVE and HAPPY in your work and/or studies!

Often barriers are hit in trying to get to the ideal, these barriers can be such things as money, resources, or perhaps most importantly not knowing with certainty what is your point **B**.

So you start moving to **C**, not the ideal, but it is OK. You are not particularly thrilled or happy, it is something you settled on doing. You have some satisfaction and sense of accomplishment, but really lack the true enthusiasm and joy you want from your job or education. And often barriers are hit in settling for **C**.

So you go to **D.** This is where you are VERY unsatisfied and unhappy in your work and/or studies. For seven years I was at a **"D"** job, getting very well paid. But I knew it was not the right professional path for me. I was very good at what I was doing, being a consultant developing training materials, documentation and marketing materials for high tech companies like Hewlett-Packard. I was making the most money I had ever made to that point in my life, but each day as I went to work I lost more and more *self-respect*. I was not really doing what I felt I was meant to do, but did not really know what that was or how to get to know what that was. I lived a constant life of un-fulfillment about my career path.

Where are you at — A, B C or D?

One time I was interviewing for a very well paying consulting job and the manager had agreed to hire me for the project. But I almost felt compelled to tell him what I really love doing and showed him a book that I had published, *HOW TO GROW A CHILD — A CHILD'S ADVICE TO PARENTS* written by my students when I was teaching in New York City. I told him I LOVE helping parents understand how to best raise their children. He saw my spark of enthusiasm which did not exist while talking about developing training programs for his organization. He decided not to hire me and he was right. I lost a potentially lucrative job, but was actually happy I did not get it, I would have been shrinking to "C" or possibly "D" if I accepted that job.

> "Your playing small doesn't serve the world. There's nothing enlightened about shrinking so that other people won't feel insecure around you."
>
> *Marianne Williamson*

Do you find yourself "shrinking" in order to maintain your job or educational standing?

Howard Schultz is the person who brought Starbucks to be the huge success that it has become. When he took over the company there were just a few locations, and now there are thousands across the globe. When he first wanted to expand he went to venture capitalists to get the needed funding. When he told prospective investors about his plan to charge $2.50, $3.50 or more for a cup of coffee, he was told, *"People won't buy your coffee when they can go down the street and get a cup of coffee for 25 cents."* He had trouble getting the money needed. But Schultz refused to compromise and lower the price. He knew he wasn't just selling a cup of coffee, he was selling a special experience. He did not shrink or compromise with what he knew was right.

What You Must Understand About Yourself

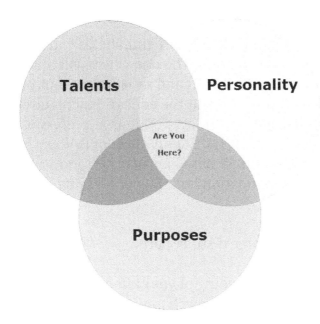

The area with in the center is the area of the best alignment, it is where one's talents, personality and purposes intersect.

There are three things you must understand about yourself, your **Talents, Personality, and Purposes**. Where these three factors converge, that is your **"B"**. I personally LOVE to sing and inspire people to action, and if you heard me sing you would be inspired to action — to walk out of the room. The talent is not there, though the purposes and personality are. I will not be able to achieve the success I want as a singer. That path would not take me to "B". You must have all three factors in alignment to achieve the success that you want.

WHAT IS THE FOUNDATIONS OF BRILLIANCE PROGRAM?

The Foundations of Brilliance program helps you determine the ideal profession for you. The one which will bring you the sense of accomplishment and satisfaction that you want. It will also help you work out the educational requirements and actions needed to perform well in that profession. Through those actions, the Foundations of Brilliance helps you build an ideal career based on a correct and strong foundation — a foundation built on your talents, personality and purposes.

The program has three distinct parts:

Part 1 is the understanding of your talents, personality and purposes. (See the upcoming chapters on each of these success factors for more information.)

Part 2 is the step where you determine the best educational or professional path to take, based on what was discovered in Part 1.

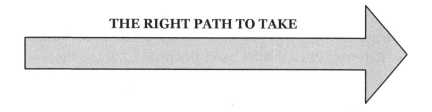

THE RIGHT PATH TO TAKE

Part 3 is the Individual Brilliance Action Plan, i.e., a plan of action to start you on the road to your ideal professional or educational program.

BRILLIANCE/ACTION PLAN

WHAT TO DO	WITH WHO	WHEN

The result of all three parts is you have discovered where you want to be brilliant and know you can achieve the brilliance as you have aligned your talents, personality and purposes.

"The reward for taking on the adventure of custom creating a profession is a life of fulfillment." Nicholas Lore

Custom creating your professional or educational activities and adventures is dependent on understanding the alignment of your talents, personality and purposes. Only then, will you truly **BE AT "B"**!

TO DO

1. Where are you, at A, B, C or D? Or are you moving to-wards or away from A, B, C or D?

2. Do you know what is your B? (We all want to Be at "B".)

3. Do you know how to get to B?

For more information please go to www.foundationsofbrilliance.com
and www.yourrightcareer.com

CHAPTER 10

YOUR PROFESSIONAL AND GLOBAL POSITIONING SYSTEMS — AND YOUR MASTERPIECE(S)

> "If you can find a path with no obsta-cles, it probably doesn't lead anywhere."
>
> *Frank A. Clark*

GABOR'S SUCCESS CERTAINTY

"The Foundations of Brilliance really gives the foundation for a productive life. My professional direction did not change so much but it gave me certainty and acknowledgment.

"And now I trust myself much more than ever and I know that I can be really good on my job and I can create a brilliant future."

YOUR PROFESSIONAL POSITIONING SYSTEM

If you have ever driven in Washington, DC you will fully understand the fear and apprehension I have when I drive in the city. I have been told, and I fully believe it, that in preparing the street plan design for Washington, DC it was done in such a way so as to confuse any invading army by getting them hopelessly lost as they try to navigate the streets. While driving in DC — sometimes when I had important meetings to attend I would get hopelessly lost. You really have to experience it to fully understand the trepidation I felt when I drove in DC.

One time in 1981, I knew I was only a few blocks from my destination, but went down a wrong street. After 25 minutes of maneuvering around the streets of DC I got out of my car and asked four different people how to get where I needed to go. Each person pointed in directly opposite directions. In desperation I called my friend David, who had a very detailed street-by-street map and he literally talked me through the streets until I arrived at my meeting. This was before the street navigational system called Global Positioning Systems [GPS] were so common.

Trying to determine an educational and professional path is very often like trying to navigate the streets of DC before there was GPS. It can be uncertain, confusing and misleading. You can get advice that will lead you in wrong directions so that you never arrive where you want to go, or get there later, much later, than you like. Wouldn't it be great to have a global positioning system with which to navigate your professional and educational directions? That is the Foundations of Brilliance program.

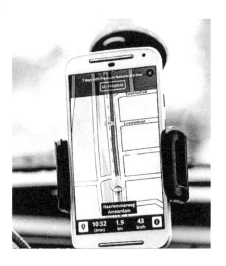

"What do I really want to do with the rest of my life?" is one of the most common questions and concerns of individuals, of all ages, most everywhere in the world. Would having a "professional or educational positioning system" be of immense value? A system that helps precisely clarify what professional or educational path best aligns with your true convictions, purposes, ambitions, talents and personality.

In my work helping individuals find their correct professional and educational path, one of the best clues that helps them precisely clarify the direction they want to go is discussing moments where they were experiencing a great sense of joy in putting out lots of effort in their work. I have often found that these experiences are marked by very strong positive feelings of personal satisfaction and success. They may even result in very vivid and detailed memories of that experience. Harnessing the personal fulfillment from these activities can help attain the result intended for a **Professional Positioning System.**

I refer to these activities as masterpieces. There is a quote I referred to earlier in Chapter 1; *"If we asked… 'What do you want to PRODUCE in life?' we could probably get a workable answer."* (*L. Ron Hubbard*) Finding examples of your masterpieces can be a major clue to help you determine what you want to produce in life and what career or educational path will best help you achieve the results you want.

EXAMPLES OF MASTERPIECES

I met with a successful professional woman who has been searching for a new direction that best aligns with who she is and what she really wants to accomplish. She told me how much she loves to dance and when I asked her about her perfect moment, her masterpiece, she mentioned a time when she was mentoring a young girl and how wonderful she felt by being able to help her. At that moment another friend came by who had created a truly marvelous school, which has a very successful music and dance program. Of course I introduced them and there was an obvious connection and a path to follow.

What is very real is that by identifying and understanding those masterpiece experiences or what was produced, you are really utilizing a **Professional Positioning System**, a system that can help you determine the path you want to go in for your career and education.

Another example is a brilliant business woman I worked with who wanted to change her direction in life. When she gave an example of a masterpiece she was really surprised by her answer. She had helped her boss get his daughter off street drugs by the advice she gave and the actions she took. This helped turn his daughter's life around in a most positive way.

She realized what she really wanted to produce!

The next day she got a totally unexpected call from someone to ask her about working with a very successful worldwide drug rehabilitation program. She realized what she wanted to do and became the president of one of their local organizations — she loves and is brilliant at what she is doing!

MY MASTERPIECE - MY PERFECT LESSON

As a teacher in New York City I taught thousands of lessons, some were great, some good, some OK and some ehhh. But one true masterpiece, my perfect lesson (I have fortunately had more than one masterpiece, but I really like this example).

It was a creative writing lesson I gave in 1969 to my fifth grade class.
I asked the class to write an essay on what the word "peace"

means to them. I told my class that for the next 20 to 30 minutes they are no longer 5th grade students, they are all to become writers. And they ALL became writers, and created their own personal writing space.

Even today almost 50 years later as I write this example I can still see the gray wintry sky as it appeared out of my classroom window; I hear the classical music that I played to create the appropriate aesthetic space; I see the beautiful lighting on the fish tank we had in our class; I see where Bruce was sitting on the floor with his back against the wall as he found his own space to write.

I remember sitting at my desk with a great sense of joy and satisfaction as I watched EVERY single child in my class stop being a student. They became writers for those 30 minutes. When I read their papers later in the day, tears came to my eyes. EVERY child met or went beyond my expectations for the quality and insightfulness of what was written.

What helped to make this a masterpiece for me is that it aligned with my talents, my personality and my purposes.

My **talents** included the ability to create a safe space where my students felt free to communicate their thoughts, as well as an ability to inspire and motivate my students to action.

My **personality** traits included my love of the arts, and how much I valued the arts as being important in the life of my students. I taught other lessons not involving the arts where everyone participated with great results and I was very proud and pleased, but that did not result in the strong emotional response I felt during the creative writing lesson.

My **purposes**, what I truly wanted to accomplish, was to inspire my students to action, thus helping to raise their level of happiness, satisfaction and pride in themselves.

My masterpiece lasted 30 minutes, some can be as short as 20 seconds. When I delivered a consultation to a young man in Russia who wanted to be a race car driver, his masterpiece was 20 seconds long. He put his car in a perfect maneuver that was both dangerous and difficult to accomplish. Some masterpieces can last for days or weeks. One 15 year-old girl related how her masterpiece took 5 years. When she was 11 she was very unpopular with the other students so she decided she would become the most popular student in school. This was accomplished when she was 15 and became the class president.

TO DO

NOTE: Examples of masterpieces (something you produced that you are very proud of) can be from any area of your life, at any age. If you have trouble finding any masterpieces, or answering the questions below, come back to this activity after completing the chapters on talents, personality and purposes.

1. Write about those things you accomplished (produced) in any area of life that gave you the level of joy and sense of fulfillment that were very special to you, i.e., your masterpieces.

1. Why would you consider them a masterpiece?

For more information please go to www.foundationsofbrilliance.com and www.yourrightcareer.com

CHAPTER 11
TALENTS

> **Talent**: The natural ability to do things well that can be developed into a greater skill.

DONALD'S SUCCESS
SINGING YOUR SONG

"You don't have to be doing poorly in life to need to do this program. If you're already 'doing fine', then ask yourself this — 'Are you at your peak performance?' If not, why not? If you want to maximize the talents and abilities that you may already recognize you have (lucky you for at least recognizing them), then you need to take a closer look at EXACTLY what it is that you are producing or creating and precisely define it. That way there is no mystery as to what it is you do when you are feeling that great feeling that you feel when you are 'Doing your thang!'...

"What a gift it is to be able to align your unique talents with your true personality [understanding what really interests you, what you value, what you love], along with a great [career] purpose in life, AND to be able to do it comfortably without any reservations."

UNDERSTANDING YOUR TALENTS

One of the great surprises to me as I began delivering the Foundations of Brilliance program was that so many people had a difficult time identifying their talents. Yet as they gained an understanding of how to identify them they were both surprised and even relieved to know how talented they were.

The definition of talent that we use is: *the natural ability to do things well that can be developed into a greater skill.*

There are three basic reasons I have observed why someone has problems identifying their talents:

1. *The viewpoint that to have a talent means you are an exceptional athlete, or have a great ability in some area of the arts.*

   Those are talents, but only certain kinds of talents. I grew up thinking I had no talent because I was not an exceptional athlete and really had minimal artistic abilities.

2. *Though you may be good at something, you don't feel you are as good as a top professional or someone who has achieved great success in an area.*

   What has to be understood is that a talent is a natural ability to do something well, THAT CAN BE DEVELOPED INTO A GREATER SKILL. If you have a natural ability in some area, through study and practice you can become a highly competent person in that area of talent. I knew of a 12 year-old girl who loved to paint. She went to New York City to meet other artists and experience what it means to be an artist. She came home and decided she did not want to paint anymore because she was not as talented as the professional artists she met. She needed to fully understand the definition of talent.

3. *What you do easily and naturally you don't think of as being a talent.*

I was working with a 17 year-old boy in Hungary, and he told me that his high school science teacher entered him in a competition to select the top physics' student in Hungary. He said other students were studying for weeks and months to get ready for the competition, but that he opened the book and started studying the day before, and he came in second in the competition. I told him how amazing that was. His response, *"Not really, anybody can do that."* I sure know I couldn't, perhaps you could, but definitely not me. To him his ability to understand and apply his knowledge in the area of physics was so natural he did not consider it to be a talent.

Another example of this is Michael, a very smart 17 year-old. When I asked him what his talents are he commented, *"I don't have any!"* (This is very typical of the type of response I get.) I asked him if he is good at anything, and he said, *"Playing video games, but I have no talents."*

My next question was, *"What talent or abilities help you at being good at video games?"* (If you are good at something you must have some talents to help you be good.) He smiled and answered, *"I have good eye-hand coordination and quick reaction time."*

I asked, *"Anything else that helps you win at video games?"*

He thought for a moment, his mouth opened wide, he gasped and said, *"I understand the game so well I can follow what is happening and predict what will happen before it happens, so I am ready for what comes next in the game."*

My response, *"So Michael, is that ability to observe and predict what will happen before it happens a talent or ability?"*

"OH YEAH!!!!!" he answered with true delight in his voice. He was on his way to developing a greater understanding of his talents.

Another example was an engineer who was asked during a seminar I delivered, *"What talents do you have?"* His response, *"That is the ruin of my life, I don't have any talents."* With further questioning he excitedly spotted a talent he had, the ability to perceive how things are working in the physical universe; he could determine if a machine was working at maximum efficiency just by observing it. Based on his perception he could fine tune the machine, he did not need any other device to help determine how efficiently it was working.

He never realized that was a talent. At the point of realization he gave such a deep sigh of recognition and relief that I thought he was going to suck all the oxygen out of the room. He wrote me several weeks later how his discovering that one talent at the seminar helped him pursue something that he never previously thought about doing.

The way I met Lee Eichenbaum, my partner in the Foundations of Brilliance program, is indicative of the problems

people have in understanding their own talents. Lee and his wife Jane (see photo) attended a seminar I was giving. As part of the seminar I had them write down a list of at least five talents they have. After a few minutes Jane called me over and said that Lee was writing his son Eric's talents instead of his own. I asked Lee what talents meant to him and he said, *"The arts and creative endeavors."* Lee, who was a successful, award winning, electrical engineer believed he had no talents. After some very fast handling of his considerations about not having any talent, Lee realized, *"I do have talent!"* That started our creating the Foundations of Brilliance together.

You can spend days and days going over all your talents, even a simple thing like the ability to write your name is a talent; perhaps not a major talent that is important to know when determining the path to take (unless you want to be a calligrapher). What I have observed is that there are certain groups of talents, they can be called categories or patterns of talents, which individuals have developed and demonstrate in their lives. These categories or patterns of talents can be applied to different areas of one's life.

Examples of the talents that a successful person would have:

- **A business person** - Good organizational skills, attention to details — what else?
- **An artist** - Creative imagination, seeing possibilities that others don't see — what else?

- **A housewife or househusband** - Able to tolerate lots of motion, able to understand the reality of their children — what else?
- **An engineer** - Problem solving, analytical thinking — what else?
- **A manager** - Leadership skills, communication skills — what else?
- **A teacher** - Make complex ideas simpler, inspire students — what else?

POSSIBLE TALENTS
SOME OF THE NUMEROUS TALENTS YOU MAY HAVE INCLUDE:

- Ability to see cause-effect consequences
- Ability to get a message across to others
- Uplift people to a happier emotional state
- To inspire
- Fast reaction time
- Able to see and understand the reality of others
- Able to create new ideas
- Ability to confront big amounts of text
- Able to organize and prioritize information
- Logical and analytical thinking
- Able to communicate ideas in writing
- High level of understanding what is being studied
- Able to apply what is being studied

- Talent to get in communication easily
- Great feeling of rhythm
- Talent to control a large group of people
- Excellent body coordination
- Demonstrating leadership by example
- Having awareness of those who are sick, sad, or downtrodden
- An ability to verbalize feelings to other people
- Creativity in bringing people together to share meaningful experiences
- Speaking publicly and inspiring large groups of people
- Ability to face adversity
- Self-Management
- Networking (direct person to person)
- Networking (virtual world)
- Critical thinking
- Decision making

- Understanding math principles
- Intuition
- Future thinking — predicting
- Analyzing the past
- Story Telling
- Project management

- To sell — To bring about understanding and close the deal
- Problem solving
- Computer literacy
- Detail orientation
- Social intelligence
- Financial management
- Polyglot (ability to learn, know many languages)
- Systems management
- Brainstorming
- Making connections between things
- Ability to focus
- Ability to handle change
- Conflict resolution

TO DO

1. Write about your talents, at least 10, and more would be helpful.

2. Think of someone who is close to you and write about their talents. How many of their talents do you also have?

3. Do you see a pattern or group of talents (e.g., to lead, to organize, to communicate, etc.)?

For more information please go to www.foundationsofbrilliance.com and www.yourrightcareer.com

CHAPTER 12
PERSONALITY

> "Everything turns out right in the end, if it isn't right, it isn't the end."
>
> *Unknown*

Personality: *The totality of somebody's attitudes, interests, behavioral patterns, emotional responses, social roles and other individual traits that endure over long periods of time.*

GEORGIA'S SUCCESS
"Right now at school I am doing very well. I just finished a research project on Oprah Winfrey and learned a lot and just started a research project on Italy. So I'm doing well at school and would just really like to say thank you for everything you did for me when you were here last, I really appreciate it.

"I have figured out a way to earn money quite fast to pay for my trip around the world in a few years, and I have also figured out what job I want to have when I'm older. I want to be an interior decorator/architect and am really excited. I can't wait to

grow up! I've figured out what school I'm going to go to get a degree in both, which is good.

"Just reading over my success story again was great because it actually made me realize how well I was doing and that I actually now (for the first time in my life) want to go to school, and want to be at school, and am really proud of myself. I know that without you and all the help you gave me I wouldn't be feeling this today. Again thank you so much!"

UNDERSTANDING YOUR PERSONALITY

DEFINITIONS

Personality - The totality of someone's attitudes, interests, behavioral patterns, emotional responses, and social roles and other individual traits that endure over long periods of time.

Attitudes - A way of thinking or feeling about someone or something, typically one that is reflected in a person's behavior. For example, I enjoy working with children; keeping the environment safe and clean is important to me, etc.

Interests - What you choose to focus your attention on and the activities you choose to be involved with. In delivering the Foundations of Brilliance program we are interested in the good positive things you choose to focus your attention on. For example, I am interested in helping parents; I love creating business ideas, etc.

Behavioral Patterns - The way in which one usually acts or conducts oneself, especially toward others. For example, some people are very outgoing and communicative, others more quiet, some are very active, others slower moving, etc.

Emotional Responses - A state of mind deriving from one's circumstances, mood, or relationships with others, situations or activities. For example, I love to spend time with my family; I really enjoy being challenged to accomplish something, etc.

Social Roles - The function assumed or part played by a person or thing in a particular social or public situation. For example, I tend to be a leader, I am an organizer, I am the person everyone trusts and seeks my advice or help, etc.

Traits - The distinguishing qualities or characteristics belonging to a person. For example, being helpful, courageous, strong willed, disciplined, etc.

Endure - To remain in existence; last. For example, think of someone you know and what can you predict about how they will act when you see them. Everyone who knows me knows I love to hug, and that trait definitely endures – if we ever meet, get ready for a BIG hug.

When I entered college I really had no idea what I wanted to major in, that is, what area of study would help me achieve what I wanted to produce to have the success in the professional and educational path that I knew was right for me. I first thought I could become a Russian translator, but that didn't work out, then I thought about becoming a psychologist, but that also didn't work out.

I finally decided I wanted to become a teacher. Why? I must admit it had nothing to do with talent or even a strong sense of purpose. My decision was mostly based on my personality – I liked the lifestyle of a teacher: I liked the long summer vacation; the Christmas and Easter holidays; I didn't have a great urge to become a millionaire, all I needed was a pre-dictable and adequate salary so I could lead a comfortable life. I knew I wanted a job where I could help others, and I did like to work with children. Thus my decision to become a teacher was based solely on my personality.

Fortunately for me I did find out I had a true talent to be a teacher, and more importantly, I realized I had a purpose that truly impelled me. I realized what I wanted to produce (students in pursuit of knowledge).

The photo on the left is of my wife (standing behind her mother), our three daughters, and my wife's sister sitting in front of her mom. My mother-in-law was 90 years old when that photo was taken, still working 20 to 30 hours a week at her business (she passed away at 95 years of age); she loved what she did, she owned a funeral home. She was mom to everyone. She had that warm caring personality and welcoming shoulder we want to find in moments of grief and loss. She very much wanted to provide that shoulder to lean on, AND SHE DID.

TENDENCY

One important clue to your personality is what do you tend to focus your attention on when you enter a new space or environment. Some people focus on the people and how they interact with each other. Others focus on how orderly the room appears, some look at how to improve the aesthetics of the space. One person said, *"I am always looking to see how safe and well protected the environment is."* When he discovered his true career purpose it had to do with helping to protect others. Another said, *"I look at the space or things in it and think how I can describe that in words?"* Her purpose aligned to being a writer.

LIST OF SOME PERSONALITY TRAITS:

- I am a good friend
- I am a pioneer (I love to start and create new things; an entrepreneur)
- I am a settler (someone who builds what others start)
- I prefer to work in a team
- I prefer to work as part of a group rather than by myself
- I love harmony
- I am a good daughter
- Money is important to me
- I must live in the city
- I always try to create peace
- I try to bring smiles to people
- I love being challenged
- I am peaceful
- I love being in communication with people
- I love making people laugh
- I always follow my beliefs
- I am a leader
- I love being a father
- I have HIGH quality standards
- I am very supportive of people
- My main interests: woodwork and travel
- I can spend 48 hours straight without sleep to organize events
- I love to bring my friends to a happier state
- I am very disciplined
- I want to have time for family
- I am sociable
- My work should be 10-15 minutes by walking from my home
- I would love to have time for family and hobbies
- I love to hug and admire others

GENERAL LIST OF PERSONALITY TRAITS[2]

Stable
Happy
Composed
Certain
Active
Aggressive
Responsible
Correctly Estimate Situations
Appreciative
High Communication Level

---

[2]
  Based on the Oxford Capacity Analysis Test

24 PERSONALITY TRAITS OF A GENIUS[3]

Which of the following personality traits do you have in common with geniuses and which do you want to further develop?

- DRIVE. Geniuses have a strong desire to work hard and long. They're willing to give all they've got to a project.
- COURAGE. It takes courage to do things others consider impossible.
- DEVOTION TO GOALS. Geniuses know what they want and go after it.
- KNOWLEDGE. Geniuses continually accumulate information.
- HONESTY. Geniuses are frank, forthright and honest.
- OPTIMISM. Geniuses never doubt they will succeed.
- ABILITY TO JUDGE. Try to understand the facts of a situation before you judge.
- ENTHUSIASM. Geniuses are so excited about what they are doing, it encourages others to cooperate with them.
- WILLINGNESS TO TAKE CHANCES. Overcome your fear of failure.
- DYNAMIC ENERGY. Don't sit on your butt waiting for something good to happen.
- ENTERPRISE. Geniuses are opportunity seekers.
- PERSUASION. Geniuses know how to motivate people to help them get ahead.
- OUTGOINGNESS. ... geniuses are able to make friends easily and be easy on their friends.
- ABILITY TO COMMUNICATE. Geniuses are able to effectively get their ideas across to others.
- PATIENCE. Be patient with others most of the time, but always be impatient with yourself.

---

[3] 1980 National Enquirer/Transworld Features

- PERCEPTION. Geniuses have their mental radar working full time.
- PERFECTIONISM. Geniuses cannot tolerate mediocrity, particularly in themselves.
- SENSE OF HUMOR. Be willing to laugh at your own expense.
- VERSATILITY. The more things you learn to accomplish, the more confidence you will develop.
- ADAPTABILITY. Being flexible enables you to adapt to changing circumstances readily.
- CURIOSITY. An inquisitive, curious mind will help you seek out new information.
- INDIVIDUALISM. Do things the way you think they should be done, without fearing somebody's disapproval.
- IDEALISM. Keep your feet on the ground, but have your head in the clouds.
- IMAGINATION. Geniuses know how to think in new combinations, see things from a different perspective, than anyone else.

SCALE OF MOTIVATION
Based on an article by L. Ron Hubbard

What motivates you? Are you truly motivated? Are you able to turn on the "ON" switch very quickly because of your level of motivation, as in the top panel in the illustration above, or are you like the bottom panel, trying all different buttons and ways to get motivated?

In terms of work and education, there are four basic levels of motivation to help you choose the direction to take. For me, I want all four points on the motivation scale!

4. Money Motivation (lowest): There is nothing evil or wrong about being motivated by money, but to get the true satisfaction and sense of accomplishment from a job or area of study, it is the lowest level. For seven years I worked at a job, and was VERY well paid. But every day I worked at that job I lost a little more self-respect. I wouldn't voluntarily tell others what I did (developing documentation and training materials for high tech companies). I knew this was not the right thing for me to do, but I was paid very well and just did it for the money.

3. Personal Gain Motivation: You are motivated by what you feel will benefit you. In Hollywood, there are many people wanting to become actors so they can have the fame and money that comes with stardom. They have no GREAT passion for acting, no real purpose beyond their own personal gain, they may not even like to act. They want the status that comes with being famous. Others work for the title of a job that brings them a level of status that is important to them. Again, there is nothing evil or wrong about being motivated by personal gain, but will that lead to a true sense of satisfaction and accomplishment from the actual work or studies that you do?

2. Personal Conviction Motivation: You have a true belief that what you are doing is the right thing for you to do. It is how you want to help and make a contribution and a difference in this world. You value what you are doing. It is what best aligns with your talents, personality and purposes.

1. **Duty Motivation (highest)**: I was delivering a seminar in Moldova (formerly part of Romania) to a group of political leaders and was discussing the Scale of Motivation. I asked if someone could define the word "duty" and a woman answered, *"If not me, who?"* You know this is what you must do, what you must take responsibility for, no matter how hard or difficult the circumstances. The Indian poet Tagore commented, *"I slept and dreamt... that life was a joy/I awoke and found...that life was duty/I acted and behold... duty was joy."*

People are often challenged to produce a high volume of work with high quality results, or find a solution to a particular problem or situation. They are promised a reward when they succeed. The reward is often money. This is appropriate in doing repetitive work, such as how many bricks can you successfully cement in a day. But when one has to use their imagination, their analytical abilities to come up with creative solutions, money is not necessarily the key motivator. What is often the greatest motivation comes from a promise of a reward that goes along with one's belief in the project they are working on, and the results they want to produce.

> "Non nobis solum nati sumus.
> [Not for ourselves alone are we born.]"
> *Cicero*

The photos above are of my daughter Kali and me. The first when she was two years old, the next taken 29 years later with the same love and affection that has lasted through the years. When Kali and my other daughters were born my wife and I knew it was our duty to be fully responsible for raising them. We were, and still are, highly motivated as parents helping our daughters create the lives they dream of having. It was and is our conviction and duty.

I have been traveling the world delivering seminars, workshops, consultations, and other promotional activities. I have been to over 40 countries. On my trips to Russia, my schedule often starts at 8:00 A.M., and I don't return to my room until 11 or 12 at night. Some days I deliver a personal consultation of up to 7 hours, and then have two presentations to give in the evening to different groups of people. On one of my trips, Katya who arranges my schedule and presentations in Russia said to me, *"Bernard we have a problem, I have scheduled you every day from 8 in the morning, until 11 at night, and forgot to schedule a time for lunch or dinner."* I LOVED IT!

I am often asked, *"Don't you find all this traveling and deliveries tiring and difficult?"* My answer is, *"NO! I love it, because I feel a great sense of duty in what I am doing."*

TO DO

Answer the following questions about some things to consider when determining your personality traits.

1. Write about your most important and valued personality traits. Which of these interest and excite you the most? Which of these do you most value?

2. Which of your talents have the greatest value and importance to you? (Your attitude about your talents is an important part of your personality; if it has great value to you these are the talents you want to use in determining your career path.)

3. What do you tend to focus your attention on when you enter a new space or environment?

4. Write about the lifestyle you would like to live.

5. Write about what you really LOVE to do.

6. What is your favorite movie or book, and why?

7. What are you passionate about (beyond what you have already written)?

The following questions are based on the Scale of Motivation, please refer to that section of the chapter that refers to the scale.

8. Write about what you would consider to be mainly *money* motivated in your life (if anything)?

9. Write about what was mainly motivated by *personal gain*? What was the personal gain you got from that?

10. Write about what you consider are your *personal convictions* that will make a positive difference for others?

11. As you read the quotes below, does anything come to mind that aligns with your *duty* and answers the question, "IF NOT ME, WHO?"

"Do your duty as you see it, and damn the consequences."
George S. Patton Jr.

"I came to realize that life lived to help others is the only one that matters and that it is my duty ... This is my highest and best use as a human."
Ben Stein

"A man does what he must — in spite of personal consequences, in spite of obstacles and dangers and pressures — and that is the basis of all human morality."
Winston Churchill

"Duty performed gives clearness and firmness to faith, and faith thus strengthened through duty becomes the more assured and satisfying to the soul."
Tryon Edwards

For more information please go to www.foundationsofbrilliance.com and www.yourrightcareer.com.

CHAPTER 13
PURPOSES

Purpose - *The definition of purpose we use is the reason for which something exists, or for which it has been done or made.*

> "When you are inspired by some great purpose, some extraordinary project, all your thoughts break their bonds: Your mind transcends limitations, your consciousness expands in every direction, and you find yourself in a new, great and wonderful world. Dormant forces, faculties and talents become alive, and you discover yourself to be a greater person by far than you ever dreamed yourself to be."
> *Patanjali*

BERNDT'S REALIZATIONS

"Getting up in the morning is so much easier." ...

"Everything makes SENSE when on purpose, one KNOWS and finds SOLUTIONS and getting up in the morning is so much easier."

What is a purpose? In reality it is a dream to pursue, a vision that impels you in your everyday activities, the reason why you want to produce, achieve and accomplish something. It is your dream of success.

What is your mission is another way of thinking about purposes.

How clearly can you state your purposes? It is more than just having the idea or concept, it is how you clearly state it in a way that truly impels you. If you don't clearly state it, you can find yourself being a wandering wonderer, wondering what you should really do for your education or career; wondering what can you REALLY accomplish with your life.

In reality every individual is limited in what they can accomplish if they don't achieve the level of skills and knowledge needed to survive in the 21st century. That includes knowing the correct path to take for their education or profession. The basic skills needed to survive in this ever-increasing technology age include: problem-solving skills; communication skills; the ability to evaluate the truth and relevance of all the data we receive; and the ability to work in groups.

But we can't minimize or overlook another area of knowledge and understanding needed to be successful, *knowing you can pursue, with confidence, your true dreams and purposes.*

Your responsibility is to ask yourself, *"Am I achieving the success I want to have?"* Then identify where you are personally lacking the skills and knowledge to help achieve that success (this assumes you know the right path to take).

To me, two of the first questions I would ask are:

   1) Do I truly know how to determine the path I want to follow to achieve my dreams and purposes?

2) Do I have the knowledge and responsibility levels needed to be able to follow that path?

When you know with certainty your TRUE career purposes and dreams, and your path to achieve those dreams, then you can truly achieve the magnificence and brilliance you want to have in your life.

Steve Jobs had a purpose that truly impelled him. What he wanted to achieve with Apple technology and products was *"... to make a contribution to the world, by making tools for the mind that advance mankind."* He most certainly achieved that through the products he inspired and helped develop at Apple.

I have personally delivered consultations to close to 1000 individuals. What I have observed is that when a person clearly identifies and states his or her purpose, the one thing they ALL have in common, no matter their age or background, is **their purpose to help in some way**. The concepts have been similar: *Help to make a difference in the lives of others; to create a beautiful space where people feel free to be themselves; help others improve conditions; help find solutions to heal the body so others can lead a happier more productive life,* and on and on.

How individuals bring this purpose to reality depends on how he or she aligns their purpose with their talents and personality. I love to inspire people to positive survival action, I love working with children, and I have the ability to get into a high level of communication and games with children easily and naturally. So I decided I would create a profession of working with and helping children. I could use the same talents and purpose in many ways, but I love working with children and created my career based on helping chil-

dren in a variety of ways (including developing the Foundations of Brilliance).

EXAMPLES OF STATED PURPOSES

As I mentioned above, when people state their basic pur-
pose(s) for their career or education the concepts have always been about how to help others in some way. What has
been interesting to me is that no two people have ever stated their purpose(s) the same way. The concepts and wording
have been similar, but each person had a unique way to
communicate what they are trying to accomplish and produce. Each statement is built on a strong understanding of
their talents, personality, and concept of their purpose(s).

Below is the wording for some of the purposes stated by
those who have received a consultation. Some are very
short, others longer, some very directly worded, others more
aesthetically stated. What they have in common is that
when stated each person saw the truth of what they were
saying and felt truly impelled by that statement to create a
positive impact in some way.

- *"To be on the communication lines of the world with truth,
  to help raise people's emotional state and inspire them to
  action."*
- *"To show people the way."*
- *"To build things that enrich people's lives."*
- *"To help people find their defining moments (an essential
  truth is clearly seen, revealed or identified)."*
- *"To make a real difference."*
- *"Through admiration help others feel good about them-
  selves."*
- *"To MAKE things go right!"*
- *"To create an emotional impact that wakes people up and
  inspires them to action."*

- *"To help bring a sane government to my country, resulting in our people being calmer, more tranquil, and in greater harmony."* (If you met this man, he is a reflection of this statement of purpose. He is so very calm and tranquil, and when I was at his home for a meeting someone dropped a paper in his kitchen; he stopped the meeting, went and picked up the paper so there would be harmony in his environment, and then returned to the meeting.)
- *"To create a beautiful and safe space, where people are free to be who they really are."*
- *"Through my writing help enlighten people to seek the truth."*
- *"To become a champion, and show people they can be a nice guy and still be a winner."* (This was the purpose of a young man, very clean cut, and nice and caring, and a martial arts champion.)
- *"To inspire others to go beyond what is expected."*
- *"To help people look better so they feel better about themselves."*

TO DO

NOTE: No Yeah Buts when answering the questions below. When delivering consultations I tell my clients I don't allow any negative thoughts or comments, we only look at what is good and right about them. I call these negative comments, "yeah buts". For example, *I would love to be a dancer, BUT my parents would object*; *I want to be a successful businessman, BUT have no experience in doing that.*

1. Take a couple of moments and write out the dreams, the big dreams, you truly want to pursue. Dreams that you know you can achieve by believing in the beauty of those dreams, AND getting the knowledge you need to make those dreams come true.

2. Look over the answers you gave earlier in the TO DO section in the chapters on global positioning systems, talents and personality (including your answers to tendency and masterpieces). Is there a statement or concept that comes to mind for your purpose?

3. If you have the concept but don't really feel impelled by the wording of the concept, work out additional wordings, choosing words you used in answering questions about your talents and personality. When you come up with the right statement you will know it. It will have a strong impact on you, you will feel impelled to get into action.

If you need additional assistance you can contact one of our consultants. Go to www.foundationsofbrilliance.com and www.yourrightcareer.com

CHAPTER 14
Now, Choose Your Path

> "Reasonable people adapt themselves to the world. Unreasonable people attempt to adapt the world to themselves. All progress, therefore, depends on unreasonable people."
>
> *George Bernard Shaw*

A mother's comment:

"[The Foundations of Brilliance] ... consult put my son on the road to creating in the Film industry. He has done camera work, created numerous videos (with pay) [one video was] #20 in the Super Bowl contest for a Doritos and Red Bull commercial. Now working with someone creating a YouTube science class for children which may be picked up for TV. He edits for that one... **He went from a protesting unfocused child to [someone following his] purpose and a winning young adult.** *Getting his Bachelor's Degree also. So proud of him and thankful for Bernard's help."*

DETERMINE YOUR IDEAL CAREER OR EDUCATION PATH

When you have determined and understood your talents, personality and purposes, including what you really want to produce, the next step is to determine what is the correct path, or paths, to take that best aligns with all these factors.

Your Right Career

Three Key Success Factors

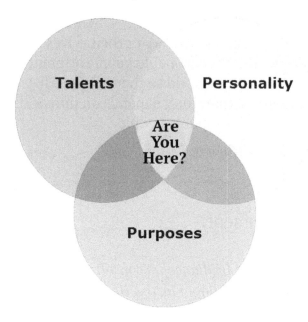

My personal statement of purpose is *"To be on the communication lines of the world with truth, to help raise people's emotional state and inspire them to action."*

This statement though it does truly impel me by itself, does not help me determine the career path to take. It is by understanding my talents (e.g., an ability to communicate through lectures, books, one-on-one consultations; my creative imagination; an ability to start new things; etc.), and understanding my personality (e.g., I love working with and helping children; I love to travel; I have a strong interest in education; I greatly value creating new friendships; and it is important to me that every 5 to 7 years I need to create new "games" to play; etc.). Understanding these three things about myself helps me determine the career and education paths to follow.

Over the last 10 years I have traveled close to one and a half million miles delivering lectures, seminars, and consultations on education, parenting, career development to thousands of people all over the world. I also had two new books published (not including this book); delivered hundreds upon hundreds of individual consultations; and so much more. I found the paths of greatest interest for me based on my talents, personality and purposes.

So how do you determine the right path to take based on your new understanding of your talents, personality and purposes? You "simply" determine what path(s) best align with all three. See the *TO DO* section at the end of this chapter.

Use the answers you wrote for the various drills throughout the book to determine what your career or educational life would be like at some point in the future. Include the lifestyle you would like to have. Put down how you really want things to be, as if you have the magical powers to create your ideal career and educational activities. After understanding your talents, personality and purposes, you should have the foundation to make this happen. It is really up to you to make it happen. (And remember you can contact us should you need help at _www.foundationsofbrilliance.com_ or www.yourrightcareer.com.)

The answers should focus on what your professional or educational life will be like.

IDEAL SCENE

"An ideal scene expresses what a scene or area ought to be. If one has not envisioned an ideal scene with which to compare the existing scene, he will not be able to recognize departure from it." L. Ron Hubbard

Below are two examples of an ideal scene (notice how the first person writes it as if it is happening). These are very comprehensive, and they align with their talents, personality and purposes.

IDEAL SCENE #1

"I am a successful and bestselling writer and author. I am an opinion leader to opinion leaders in industry, business, government, the arts. I am in demand as a speaker; mostly, people come to me at my safe haven, but when I do travel, it is always first class...

"My retreat... is a beautiful, peaceful, and inspiring place. It has a hacienda, stables and horses, fruit and other trees, a pool, spa, patios on a large property. There are also aviaries, fish ponds, dogs and cats. The cuisine is superb and very healthy. I have my own special horse — a Paso Fino — whom I ride and enjoy thoroughly. Through my ranch, I am also able to promote the breed...

"I am able to help bring together people of goodwill from all sectors who then work together to solve society's ills.

"Through these efforts, conditions rapidly improve in the areas influenced by these [leaders]. We see this in better working conditions, people becoming [more aware and happier], more help emanating from individuals within these groups... More people

are flourishing and prospering and they, in turn, have a positive impact on their individual spheres of influence...

"We are ... helping keep this planet and Mankind within it surviving into the future sufficient to salvaging it.

"Money is simply not ever an issue. I have an abundance of it. I have people managing it who know how to turn every dollar into more value for myself and others... All my books are bestsellers. I am a columnist for a major media outlet...

"... I am a catalyst for improvement and change among such people.

"Life is rather effortless ... Together, we are an unstoppable force for good."

IDEAL SCENE #2

"The way to get the most 'bang' from my work is to use my talents (the abilities to permeate, observe, learn, educate) and to utilize them actively, pushing to have a positive impact rather than just going through the motions or going along with the flow.

"My wealth will not be an accumulation of cash flow, but an accumulation of investments that will generate a significant return over time. The investments will vary in the amount of money and time committed.

"No individual job, or investment, will be all-consuming. I need the freedom to... be with my family (as more than just a bystander), and to help others in their lives and activities (my friends, or people who are friends to mankind)...

"Permeate. Improve. Those are the watchwords.

"Others will respect me for my contributions, my morale will be high, and the activities will succeed better because of my help.

"When I tell others about my products and investments, they'll think 'Wow, smart; I'd like that too in my activities or my investment portfolio.' And they'll share their ideas, because they want my participation.

"In terms of the businesses I'm intimately involved in, they [will] deliver a good product or service to others, a product I can be proud of (reduces cost, gets better results, good for environment or good for life, etc.)."

When you come up with a direction you may have to do additional research to determine the specific path to follow. For example, I was working with a 16 year-old who realized he wanted to be an engineer, but wasn't sure what type of engineering he wanted to study. He began to research the different types of engineering fields he could go into that best matched his talents and personality.

TO DO

Use the answers you wrote for the various drills throughout the book to determine what your career or educational life would be like at some point in the future. Put down how you really want things to be, as if you have the magical powers to create your ideal career and educational activities.

1. Write about the career or education path(s) that aligns with your talents (e.g., if you are good at learning languages, perhaps become a translator, etc.).

2. Write about the career or education path(s) that aligns with your personality (e.g., if you love working with children, perhaps a teacher or opening a daycare center, etc.).

3. Write about the career or education path(s) that aligns with your purposes and what you want to produce (e.g., you want to create works of art that inspire others).

4. Write out possible career path(s) based on 1 to 3 above; then determine which path(s) best aligns with YOUR talents, personality and purposes (e.g., *purpose* - to help bring others into the area of the arts, *talents* - wonderful dancer and teacher, *personality* - love working with children and creating a business. Perhaps opening a children's dance school best aligns with these talents, personality traits and purposes).

5. Write out how your professional life would be at some time in the future based on 1-4 above, write it out as if it is happening. Include the lifestyle you would like to have (e.g., I want a career that allows me lots of freedom to spend time with my family; I want to have time to travel as part of my work, etc.).

6. Ensure your ideal scene aligns with your talents, personality and purposes; for example: you have no talent for singing, but want to start a career as a singer, or you love working in ways directly interacting and helping people, but you decide to work as an accountant that will focus your time and energies in a way to keep you from directly interacting and helping others.

If you need additional assistance you can contact one of our consultants. Go to www.foundationsofbrilliance.com and www.yourrightcareer.com

CHAPTER 15
ACTION PLAN

> "Life is action and passion, it is required of a man that he should share the passion and action of his time, at peril of being judged not to have lived at all."
>
> *Oliver Wendell Holmes*

Christian wrote,

"After two hours of consultation we managed to define and narrow down the purpose 100% ... I mean not just 99.5%... I mean ONE HUNDRED PERCENT TOTALLY DEFINED which gave release in the form of grief and a feeling of once more being at home! We succeeded in taking away false things that APPEARED to be part of the purpose, but wasn't, and we got the true purpose revitalized.

*"It is part of my purpose to create courses that facilitates learning, so that the acquisition of a subject becomes easy, fast and fun. Right now I am making the finishing touches on a big mathematical course that goes from the very bottom to the final exam of high school. A lot of students have done the course with great success. What they couldn't learn in school for years, they learned in weeks or just a few month on this course. Now it is being translated into English, Russian, Czech, Dutch and other languages. Thousands of hours of work has been spent on creating this course, and **I would have given up, if it had not been in alignment with my purpose revitalized during the consultation with Bernard.** Thanks for your help!"*

Based on all that you have done and the direction(s) you have decided to pursue, the final step is to write a very basic action plan on what you will do to get started in applying what you have learned about yourself.

Write out what are the main things you have to do to start on the journey to living the life you imagine. This can be as simple as steps to take and actions to complete in order of priority.

When I left teaching in 1976 and moved from New York City to Los Angeles I wanted to get involved in Children's Television and writing books, both of which I knew very, very little about, and had absolutely no experience. I began to find resources to get the knowledge I needed:

- I bought books

- Researched in libraries

- Attended conferences and adult education courses about both topics

- Started to write books

- Created a concept for a children's television show

- Met people who could help (One very successful action was sitting up front at conferences or any class I took, and asked questions of the speaker; then afterwards going up to the speaker and introducing myself and getting their contact information. This directly led to my becoming a creative consultant for a children's television show.)

- In 6 years I had four books published

A book I recommend is *The Natural Laws of Management* by Arte Maran (www.naturallawsblog.com). This book provides the tools to coordinate and align your actions and energies that will help you succeed at achieving the satisfaction and fulfillment you want from your education and career.

TO DO

Here is a basic outline for creating your Action Plan. Start with whatever steps that seem right for you, begin RIGHT NOW, to take responsibility for the career and education path you want to pursue:

1. Determine the knowledge you need to pursue your ideal path; then determine how and where you can get that knowledge (school, internet, people you know who can help, etc.). Start to get that knowledge.

2. Determine what are the resources you will need to follow your path (people to work with, how much money, what materials, etc.). Start to gather those resources or learn where they are available.

3. Start to create or participate in the "game" you want to play. For example, start working in the area of your chosen profession. Find an internship or volunteer, begin to create any relevant product (start writing that book you want to write, or paint the painting, or selling a product on the internet, etc.).

If you need additional assistance you can contact one of our consultants. Go to www.foundationsofbrilliance.com and www.yourrightcareer.com

CHAPTER 16
WHAT'S NEXT?

"Destiny is not a matter of chance; it is a
matter of choice. It is not a thing to be
waited for, it is a thing to be achieved."
William Jennings Bryan

We invite you to visit our websites at:

www.foundationsofbrilliance.com
and
www.yourrightcareer.com

On the sites you can see which of our products and services could best meet your needs or those of people you know.

This includes taking our online training course, finding a career choice specialist in your area of the world who can help you with a private consultation, additional information about our career and educational choice programs and read further testimonials from people around the world.

We want you to experience the joy and sense of personal fulfillment that comes from going confidently in the direction of your dreams and living the life you only dare to imagine.

If you need any further assistance or if you have any questions or comments, please send us an email at: bernard@yourrightcareer.com or lee@yourrightcareer.com.

Remember, "*Everything turns out right in the end, if it isn't right, it isn't the end!*"

APPENDIX

PROFESSIONAL CATEGORIES[4]

The following list was found on a website to help people decide on the potential professional and educational paths that are best for them.

As you look over the list and if you find a career that interests you and you need to get more reality on, ask yourself these five basic questions:

- What are the talents needed to be brilliant at that career?
- What are the personality traits that align with being brilliant in that career?
- How can that career help you achieve your true career purpose(s)?
- Where would you be on the Scale of Motivation (money, personal gain, personal conviction, duty) when choosing that career path?
- Do you want to be truly brilliant in that career?

---

[4] skillcow.com

Arts / Design / Fashion

3-D Animator
3-D Object Modeler
Actor
Animator
Architect
Art Director
Artist/Illustrator
Assistant Designer
Audio Film Editor
Audio/Sound Engineer
Autocad Technician
Automotive Designer
Broadcaster
CAD Design Engineer
Choreographer
Cinematographer
Civil Engineer
Commercial Artist
Computer Graphics Special-
  ist
Dancer
Decorator
Designer
Desktop Publisher
Digital Artist
Digital Media Specialist
Digital Video/Sound Editor
Fashion Designer
Fashion Events Manager
Fashion Merchandiser
Film Producer
Film Producer Assistant
Floral Designer
Game Designer

Glamour Photographer
Graphic Designer
Industrial Designer
Industrial Engineer
Interior Designer
Jeweler
Journalist
Landscape Architect
Media Buyer
Motion Picture Director
Musician
Photographer
Producer
Publisher
Radio/TV Announcer
Singer
TV Programmer
Technical Illustrator
Theatrical Director
Urban Planner
Web Designer

Aviation

Aerospace Engineer
Air Traffic Controller
Aircraft Maintenance Tech-
  nician
Airframe & Power Plant
  Technician
Flight Attendant
Flight Engineer
Pilot

Beauty

Barber

Cosmetologist
Hair Stylist
Manicurist
Skin Care Consultant

Business

Accountant/CPA
Acquisition Analyst
Administrative Analyst
Advertising Manager
Auditor
Banker
Bookkeeping Clerk
Business Analyst
Business Planner
Business Programmer
Buyer/Purchasing Agent
Cash Manager
Collection Manager
Compensation Analyst
Controller
Consumer Relations Mana-
  ger
Contract Administrator
Copywriter
Corporate Planner
Credit/Loan Manager
Cruise Director
Cryptologist
Database Admin (DBA)
Diamond Merchant
Direct Marketer
Distribution Manager
Economist
Employment Agent

Entrepreneur
Escrow Officer
Executive Assistant
Executive Recruiter
Financial Analyst
Financial Planner
Financier
Forensic Accountant
Franchise Management
Fund Raiser
Funeral Director
General Manager
Golf Club Manager
Home Economist
Hotel Manager
Human Resource Manager
Importer
Insurance Adjuster
International Accountant
Investment Banker
Investment Manager
Labor Negotiator
Labor Organizer
Labor Relations Manager
Loan Officer
MIS Manager/Director
Management Consultant
Marketing Analyst
Marketing Manager
Materials Manager
Medical Investor
Medical Receptionist
Merchandiser
New Product Specialist
Office Manager
Payroll Manager

Personnel Specialist
Private Banker
Product Manager
Production Planner
Production Support
Property Manager
Receptionist
Recreational Director
Relocation Manager
Research Specialist
Sales Engineer
Sales Manager
Sales Promotion Manager
Sales Representative
Sales Trainer
Salesperson
Secretary
Securities Analyst
Security Consultant
Security Director
Special Events Manager
Sports Event Manager
Stockbroker
Tax Specialist
Telecom Analyst
Telemarketer
Title Examiner
Tour Escort
Tour Guide Director
Travel Agent
Underwriter
Works Director

Criminal Justice
Bankruptcy Attorney
Border Patrol Agent
Correctional Officer
Detective
Development Officer
Hearing Officer
Homeland Security Officer
International Lawyer
Investigator
Law Enforcement Officer
Lawyer
Legal Nurse Consultant
Legal Secretary
Paralegal
Parole Officer
Private Investigator
Probation Officer

Culinary Arts
Baker/Pastry Chef
Chef/Gourmet Chef
Pastry Sous Chef
Restaurant Manager
Viticulturist
Winemaker

Education
Child Care Manager
Day Care Counselor
Education Administrator
Preschool Management
Preschool Teacher
Professor/Instructor
Rabbi/Minister

Special Ed Teacher
Teacher
University Administrator
University Dean

General Arts and Sciences

Geologist
Sanitation Engineer
Scientific Programmer
Scientific Writer

Health Care / Human Services

Addictions Counselor
Biofeedback Specialist
Cardiology Technologist
Certified Nurse
Certified Nurse Aide
Chemical Dependency Specialist
Chiropractor
Clinical Medical Assistant
Clinical Research Assistant
Dental Assistant
Dental Hygienist
Dentist
Doctor
EKG Technician
Family Counseling Manager
Geriatric Specialist
Gerontologist
HMO Administrator
Health Care Manager

Health Care Reimbursement Specialist
Health Claims Examiner
Health Information Technician
Health Service Administrator
Health Therapist
Health Unit Coordinator
Hospital Administrator
Medical Assistant
Medical Coding & Billing Specialist
Medical Office Assistant
Medical Secretary
Medical Technician
Mental Health Counselor
Nursing Administrator
Occupational Therapist
Optical Technician
Optometrist
Outplacement Counselor
Patient Care Technician
Pharmacist
Pharmacy Technician
Physician
Physician's Assistant
Podiatrist
Radiologic Technician
Radiology Manager
Registered Nurse
Rehabilitation Counselor
Speech Pathologist
Stress Reduction Specialist
Veterinarian
X-Ray Technician

Liberal Arts / Traditional University

Actuary
Agricultural Inspector
Agricultural Scientist
Anthropologist
Astronomer
Author
Biologist
Biotech Researcher
Chemical Engineer
Chemist
City Housing Manager
City Manager
Community Affairs Manager
Community Support
  Worker
Editor
Environmental Analyst
Environmental Attorney
Environmental Specialist
Fish/Wildlife Specialist
Forestry Technician
Freelance Writer
Hazardous Waste Manager
Horticulturist
Interpreter
Lab Technician
Library Manager
Lobbyist
Marine Biologist
Mathematician
Meteorologist
Microbiologist
Nuclear Engineer
Nuclear Specialist
Oceanographer
Park Ranger
Petroleum Engineer
Physicist
Planning Specialist
Political Analyst
Political Scientist
Politician
Public Administrator
Public Relations Specialist
Social Director
Social Researcher
Social Scientist
Social Worker
Sociologist
Soil Scientist
Speech Writer
Statistician
Surveyor
Technical Writer
Translator
Tree Surgeon
Union Representative
Writer

Massage / Wellness

Athletic/Pro Coach
Dietitian
Fitness Consultant
Fitness Instructor
Health Fitness Specialist
Holistic Health Practitioner
Massage Therapist

Nutritionist
Personal Fitness Trainer
Physical Therapist
Professional Athlete
Trainer

Technology / Computer / IT

A+ Certified Configuration Associate
Biomedical Engineer
Cisco Certified Operations Technician
Cisco Network Engineer
Computer Engineer
Computer Hardware Technician
Computer Operator
Computer Programmer
Computer Support Specialist
Computer Systems Technician
Computer Technical Support Help Desk
Construction Engineer
Engineer Technician
Environmental Engineer
Help Desk Technician
IT Support Specialist
Mechanical Engineer
Network Admin
Network Engineer
PC Support Specialist
Software Engineer
Systems Analyst

Systems Engineer
Systems Programmer
Webmaster

Trade

AC & Refrigeration Technician
Animal Trainer
Appraiser
Auto Repair Technician
Building Contractor
Building Inspector
Building Manager
Cashier
Ceramic Engineer
Courier
Developer
Electrical Designer
Electrical Engineer
Electro-optical Engineer
Electronics Engineer
Estimator
Facilities Manager
Fast Food Manager
Gemologist
Groundskeeper
HVAC Maintenance Technician
International Courier
Land Developer
Metallographic Technician
Metallurgical Engineer
Motorcycle Technician Specialist
Quality Control Inspector

Railroad Engineer
Real Estate Broker
Redevelopment Specialist
Retail Store Manager
Safety Engineer
Seminar Presenter
Service Manager
Structural Engineer
Traffic Manager
Workshop Presenter

Made in the USA
Las Vegas, NV
26 July 2022

52185104R10075